THE FEATHER LADDER

pictureshowpress.net

Cover Art: Cindy Rinne

FIRST EDITION

ISBN-13: 979-8-9850690-0-6

The Feather Ladder

CINDY RINNE

Picture Show Press

for Alan Van Fleet and Edgar Perez Peña

POEMS

III The Climb

I

Creatures of the Wind

Almost Grown

carved dots and dashes

on a triangle shape

with rounded edges

amber amulet

for his necklace

to keep evil spirits away

Creatures of the Wind

In ancient times, several birds met around a fire circle of stones,
their beaks distorted in the flames. Sparks landed near
the eagles' talons. They discussed how can they show their unity?
Also, how to connect earth to sky for humans?

They spend their lives walking around
to the exact same spot.

Goose had a vision of The Feather Keeper standing on raven's head. He held the sun. But goose kept silent. Then suggested they donate feathers to create a ladder to the sky.

A silent flyer swept past as dawn streaked the fir trees.

Tricksters

Hyena overheard
The birds' exchange
Fumbled down the steep
Embankment needled
In blazing dawn
Sun. Raven
Clipped
His large ear.
Blood curled in
Sharp teeth. Raven flew
In chalked figure
Eights, *caw-caw*
Mocking the
Feline's yell.

The Oracle

The birds described

Dove, eagle, raven, and goose hastened to find
The Feather Keeper. He greeted them and smiled.
The Feather Keeper observed with oracle eyes
embodying male and female energies.
Wore a deerskin shirt with bird's ribs
hand-sewn into it, leggings
with painted feathers, and elk skin moccasins.
A necklace – snail shells, amber, claw
of roe deer, and wild boar teeth.
He was small in stature, but strong and agile.
Two long braids cascaded down his back –
One for golden sun
The other for silver moon.

their plan to the child.

Generations

The Feather Keeper slept in trees.
Had the power of wind and air.
        Protection of the sky.

Casted nets from tree-to-tree
to capture floating feathers
        as they washed over him.

Held them in a beaded pouch.
Gave to cave artists for brushes,
        others to leaders for headdresses,

and to Shamans to ward off sickness.
In a year's cycle, The Feather
        Keeper traveled from desert

to mountains like his father.
He had never removed
        a feather from a bird's body.

The Feather Keeper understood

nature and creatures had souls. He trusted elk
to guide him because they knew the mysteries
of the forest. But the boys teased him:

You spend all your time in trees talking with birds
and love a man. We are strong like osprey. Come, hunt ibex.

I trusted you as friends. I love a hunter from another tribe.
What is that to you? I know our leader can be cruel,
but don't take it out on me.

Lynx stood between them. She said to the teasing boys:

You showed your true self. As nomads you are equal
and each have talents to help the tribe. He has hidden
knowledge and will be a healer.

Owl

The birds desired to give live feathers

bringing their energy to the ladder.

The Feather Keeper thanked them for this truth.

He began to remove feathers from dove,

eagle, raven, and goose as if pulling a splinter from his finger.

Owl observed this strange occurrence.

Glided overhead three times. He coasted higher

and higher until he almost disappeared against the wind.

He cried out of the dusk:

Spirits of dead animals and humans
have great power. You have forgotten
the owls who guide spirits
to the Underworld, the keepers
of the sacred knowledge.

Left out of the plan, owl vanished.

Invitation

The Feather Keeper invited sparrow and hawk

to represent fertility and earth wisdom.

Hawk offered extra feathers for each bird to paint

their sky symbol.

The Feather Keeper scooped the feathers for cleansing.

Clear Sky

I

Talons, claws, and beaks grasped clusters of feathers
from The Feather Keeper's arms. He delighted in the flapping

like drum rhythms. The birds delivered the feathers
to a gourd bowl in a river gorge. As the feathers soaked,

hawk carved spirals, circles, and etched a ladder into the cliff wall.
In a wooden cradleboard, Wild Horse cried.

Distracted hawk sang, *Hush little baby.*
Clear Sky, his mother with flowing hair, smiled.

Wondered why feathers from so many birds rested in the bowl.
Hawk's voice echoed through the valley as she shared

the feather ladder story.

II

Clear Sky warned the birds they have three days of sun, then the sky
will grow angry with sparks and thunderclaps.

III

Goose delegated the tasks –
goose, sparrow, dove, and raven

to transport the wet feathers.
Hawk to seek a red stag deer.
Eagle to collect pine needles.

We will meet at the red rocks of the Desert Tribe.

Clear Sky chanted a river blessing
over the winged ones.

Ancestors Danced

Eagle migrated to the lands of the Ice Tribe.
Diffused patches of light sparkled on his wings.
Among the greenish glow of the northern lights
The Ancestors danced in the next life.

Seal-skin boots stomped and turned on a floor lit by stars.
Eagle thanked the sky for this gift of colors.
Asked the Sitka Spruce if he could gather
Pine needles to wrap around the joints

Of the feather ladder?
The pine scent made him dizzy.
He ceased motion perched on the rough skin.

I will give my spiky needles to you.
First, listen to the story
Of what is below my raised roots.
The history of the Tree Tribe had its
Origins when the frozen land was warm.
Our language was born
Of earthquakes; growing our roots deep.

Eagle stretched and saw evidence below the tree's roots
Of duckbilled and polar dinosaurs who endured
Months of cold and dark.
Then wooly mammoths caught in permafrost.
The cave lion of rounded ears, tufted tails, and tiger-like stripes.

Layers of migratory caribou with fur and a dense undercoat.
Thanked spruce for its needles and the history of ice told by bones.

Thunder Sun

In the vast, cloudless sky over empty golden fields

hawk floated.

A shadow loomed with large antlers.

Red stag deer appeared – they lingered, tasted earth.

Hawk canvassed several of the herd to find one willing

to donate themselves for sinew and a bone needle.

No one responded.

Hawk followed a trail of spotted eagle feathers

to an elderly deer at the edge of the herd.

His fur matted beneath his neck.

A broken arrow stuck in his side.

The dried grasses below him spelled, *Today*.

Hawk saw many suns in red stag deer's eyes.

One sun had rays of feathers.

The deer's voice rumbled,

Today is the day for prophecy to be fulfilled.
I give my life so others may touch the heavens.
Collect an osprey feather. The climber is to wear
this feather for his eyes not to be blinded by the sun.

Stone Woman

I

Sparrow drifted down to the aroma of autumn sage

grasping wet feathers. Her blue-black eyes

grabbed sparrow. Stone Woman held sacred fire in one hand,

a staff of antlers incised with motifs in the other.

She read the engravings.

There is one willing to climb your ladder of feathers and pine.
He must pass this test to discover his origin.

Sparrow ate some berries, nodded to the Stone Woman,

and dashed to nearby rocks. Goose, dove, and raven

joined sparrow, carrying the rest of the wet feathers.

Raven brought the light of dawn glowing from red to ochre

on the rounded rocks to dry them.

II

Stone Woman watched as cave paintings

of calf, osprey, stag, and bear

whirled off the walls

rested in a circle around her.

She had saved one flame,

  a sacred flame,

    inner fire –

  sun in her hand.

(Ancestors spoke through bear)

One day your child of feathers,
  seeking sky,
    a breath –
will hold the sun.

The Underworld

Owl swooped down under blackened moon.

Stole some of the cleansed feathers

to hide them in the Underworld.

***

Dove, raven, goose, and sparrow panicked at the missing feathers

like beads falling off a buckskin shirt.

They found owl's pellet. Cried out to The Feather Keeper,

Come and bring peace.

The Feather Keeper found a cave

with a dark hole near the entrance –

a portal to the Underworld.

He begged owl,

I come on behalf of the birds.
They want the feathers
of the one who takes a freed soul
from the physical world
to the realm of the spirit.
As a part of the feather ladder,
allow me to pluck some of your feathers
to cleanse them
in wild grasses and water.

Owl Turned

Owl offered his feathers to the birds.

The Feather Keeper's hands became invisible like spirit

as they thrusted through the cave floor. He retrieved
the stolen feathers

and owl's feathers. They rose through the smooth stone.

Owl responded,

Owl magic to protect your skin.
It will be as night to your fingers.

The Feather Keeper did not understand.

II

Ancient Wings

A Gift for His Lover

The Feather Keeper grasped the amber bead

To begin the necklace.

Raised it to capture the sun.

A glow filled the cavern.

Next, two fish vertebrae threaded.

Roe deer claw slid into the center.

Two more fish vertebrae and an amber bead

Completed the design.

Tightened the knot.

Fire hissed smoke.

He prayed in soft, clear tones –

Spirit of deer, bestow the wearer
of this necklace with strength and tenderness.

He prepared to leave.

Bear would awaken and want his cave back.

The Gateway

Dove painted each hawk feather with its own sky symbol.

Dove and goose suspended a thin rope
between two white oak trees.

The boy knotted the painted feathers every four inches.

They hung like ringing bells in the evening breeze.
Hyena grunted and pawed through the darkness.

He leapt to tear down the painted garland with his teeth.

It ribboned around his legs.
He stomped and cracked feathers.

Humans were not meant to fly.

The leader hid nearby and smiled.

The birds returned to find
trampled feathers,
tried to save what they could of hawk's gift.

Goose declared,
Owl, come as a guardian.

We need to build the feather ladder now,
Raven fumed.

A New Resolve

The Feather Keeper joined the birds in the desert,
placing the stolen feathers
and the owl's cleansed feathers on heated rocks.
Hawk delivered sinew, bone needle, and an osprey feather.
Eagle placed the pine needles in a clay bowl.

Sparrow told them they needed other animals
to help before the storm crashed around them.
She asked bees and sheep
for honey and water to soak the pine needles,
making them pliable for bending around the ladder's joints.

Bees circled and said,

Ancient wings to change
the world of feathers.

Rook Bones

Owl descended as the wind rustled in the oak trees.

He beseeched the birds,

Search for rook bones as a sign.
Construct the ladder there
and hope the impossible will occur.

The climber will be light as a newborn.

A snake slithered under a dark red rock.

Dove noticed spires of yellow sandstone
carved like humans
and rook bones in a circle.

Goose directed raven and hawk

to weave the smaller feathers as the seven rungs.

Eagle held the largest for outside supports.

Sparrow wanted that job

which caused her vision to blur,

nervous the ladder would not survive the sun.

Eagle's skin pricked by the heat,

as he glared through sparrow to the bone.

Goose tried not to smolder and guided sparrow,

> *Carefully thread the bone needle,*
> *secure the sides to the rungs.*
> *Dove will twist pine needles around the joints.*

The ladder formed rectangles

like deer stacked one upon another

from earth to sky.

No Resistance to Air

The Feather Keeper skimmed granite rocks.

Bent down

and removed the darkened quill off a large stone.
He rested on the coolness of the boulder.

Feather upright in his hand,

he inhaled and exhaled slow, deep breaths.
Studied the shaft thinned down to a stem.

Stark as his hair,

the barbs at the base like waves.
Larger afterfeathers curved into the vane.

Vanes had split,

survived opposing winds.
The Feather Keeper brushed it next to his ear.

Listened.

He held the quill sideways; it offered no resistance to air.
Lingered on the gusts,

the movement of raven.

Chills raced through his body as he sensed a circular truth,
his life wrapped around creatures of the nest.

III

The Climb

Decisions

From a parched tree bone gulley
woven cotton clouds levitated
forming an image of hawk
sent out to signal the tribes

gathering all peoples to sacred ground.
Lynx attended as a witness.

Arriving through the scent
of pine needles,
raven stitched the circle of birds' reasons
to the tribes for cultivating a feather ladder.

Raven asked the tribes
to choose those who would ascend.

The plains tribe decided the sky was too far.
Ice tribe, the ladder too fragile.
Mountain tribe safer on solid ground.

Hyena giggled, delighted
as the birds'
plan diffused.

The Feather Keeper

bolted into the fray,

burn sage.
I will climb.

Still, the boys teased him,

Now you think you can fly.
Spears and arrows our tools,
not a weak ladder rejected by the tribes.

Presents

Birds and tribes chattered at the same time

about The Feather Keeper's decision

to climb the ladder.

Brought presents to prepare him.

Wings of feathers fastened to his arms with leather bands.

His face painted.

The osprey feather inserted into his hair.

Skin fused

with sage smoke.

Ascension

A deep breath. He began to climb.

Overlapping barbs cut his feet.

Blurred the reason he embarked on this journey.

A creek burbled.

He watched

Hyena's ears grow even taller.

Tail a tuft.

Fangs dissolved.

Turned into a rabbit.

The Feather Keeper ascended as a layer of silence settled

Into the vertical, dark lines of the cliffs.

The boys taunting forgotten like a healed wound.

The Climber's Thoughts

Sometimes I desired to exchange my life
with other boys, trapping to hunt.
But I know the winged-ones.
Their dream became mine.

Dissolutions

Wind Spirit swirled

Clear Sky noticed snow falls

Quills

    Tickling

        Her skin

Neither cold nor wet

Hawk's voice resonated

Off sacred spires

    The ladder

        Our ladder

Birds and tribes glanced toward the sky

A collective gasp

The ladder coming apart

As The Feather Keeper

Went past each rung

Totem Guide

The ladder vibrated
under The Feather
Keeper's feet
like an avalanche.
His sweat mixed into a cloud
of ice crystals. Afraid,
he called upon
goat animal guide,

Please help me
reach the sun.

A black blur shifted
outside his
sight. Giant raven
flew higher.
Spread his wings,
becoming the top
rung of the ladder.

Climb up here on
my head.

Touched the Sun

The Feather Keeper scraped

        his way up

protected by osprey's feather

from the brilliance of the sun,

he thanked goat and raven

        for their help.

Recalled owl magic sealing

his skin from the heat,

proclaiming him

light as a newborn.

He held the sun in his outstretched arms.

The sun said,

This was your house.
Your origin above
where birds
raised their young.
You were born
            of water by clouds.
They brought you here
to live on fire.
Eagle bore you downward
through the air
to dwell with the nomadic tribes.
You climbed the ladder
completing
            the elemental circle.

Truth

Trembling,

The Feather Keeper

Knew as blood coursed

Through his body

And in the magical place

Of spirit,

He had once lived

On the sun.

The Offering

I give you a meteorite

To deepen

Your spiritual roots

Honor this force of nature

Once a shooting star

Survived the burning

Receive guidance

Trust your inner voice

Now connected to the universe

Heal and teach

Sharing this clarity with others.

Fire Stone

The Feather Keeper spoke,

Thank you for the offering.
I will cherish this fire stone
and share wisdom gained
with the tribes.
   Also, thank you
for letting me live with you in the past.

The sun said,

During the daytime I watched your travels
and the moon observed
your sleep.
         Now it is time
for you to return to earth.

Invisible

Hunter from another tribe looked up

caressed his roe deer claw necklace.
Strength filled his limbs.

I am made of feathers too.

A Meteorite

Cloud rays sliced the air

shined in four directions.

The sun as center

spokes with an outer circle of feathers

as The Feather Keeper returned

Goose said,

You came back with a new way
for humans to touch the sky

The Feather Keeper replied,

Feathers for healing
a stone from the stars
and the sun's energy
as I learn the Shaman's ways

With my lover
No more teasing

Remembering always the wisdom
and patience of a circle of birds

That is why, to this day, the elemental preserves a world of nests

ACKNOWLEDGEMENTS

I am grateful to the following literary magazines in which these poems first appeared, some in a slightly different form:

Mojave River Review: “Tricksters”

Mystic Nebula: “No Resistance to Air” and “Totem Guide”

Twelve Winters Press: “Ancestors Dance”

Written by Veterans, Anthology #4: “Creatures of the Wind,” “The Oracle,” “Generations,” “Owl,” “Invitation,” and “Clear Sky”

Young Ravens Literary Review: “Touch the Sun”

CINDY RINNE creates fiber art and writes in San Bernardino, CA. Represented Poet by Lark Gallery, LA, CA. A Pushcart nominee, her poems have appeared in literary journals, anthologies, art exhibits, and dance performances. Cindy is the author of several books: *Words Become Ashes: An Offering* (Bamboo Dart Press), *Today in the Forest with Toti O'Brien* (Moonrise Press), *silence between drumbeats* (Four Feathers Press), *Knife Me Split Memories* (Cholla Needles Press), *Letters Under Rock with Bory Thach* (Elyssar Press), and others. Her poetry appeared or is forthcoming in: *The Closed Eye Open*, *Wild Roof Journal*, *Thimble Literary Magazine*, *Verse-Virtual*, and elsewhere. Find out more about Cindy at www.fiberverse.com.

www.ingramcontent.com/pod-product-compliance
Lightning Source LLC
LaVergne TN
LVHW090538110826
845146LV00003B/1160

* 9 7 9 8 9 8 5 0 6 9 0 0 6 *